D1618568

High Shelf

High Shelf Issue VIII 4.10.19
Portland, Oregon.
Copyright 2019, High Shelf Press

ISBN: 978-1-7330279-7-7

Cover Image by Lynn Hanley
Design and Layout by C. M. Tollefson
Edited by David Seung & C. M. Tollefson

High Shelf X

September 2019

"... My bud opens
splashing red
and you depart,
stinger sheathed... "

Josephine Pino

"...The spectacle of their unveiling

Desire. Here, everything

Makes a name out of its absence..."
Ronnie Festok

Table Of Contents

Window Washers

Beth Morris

Before the scaffolding came down,
workmen straddled the skyscraper.
Fearless artists with rags, sprays,
and squeegees. Masterpiece restorers
erasing the amateur touch-up
from the surface of a painting
found in an old farmer's attic,
revealing an Eakins or Grandma Moses
under the grime, construction dust,
smoke from factories carried by wind
and rain across the harbor.
Each pane of glass transformed
into a crystal reflecting sunlight
off the river's tides.

Before the Towers came down,
the window washers
could not imagine
their workmanship would enable
the pilots to pinpoint their targets.
Expose the office workers
behind the casements
to their approaching death,
from both sides of the glass.
They could only watch
their artistry descend,
decay return;
debris, dust,
and ash.

Lines & Shadows
Jeremiah Gilbert

Everyone Is There When We Look

Richard Stuart Perkins

XL

Because America – this is me.
This is my distillation: particulates fragile and earthen,
Bounding, an amalgamation of fragments.

Because America, I am young, and want to know a thousand things, and never kneel or
pray when advised,
Because between me and God swings a whip and a hammer,
A life defining slap upon my ass,
The uncivil slap upon my face.

Because America,
Africa shadows me,
Uneasy in her shade,
Beyond her outline a harsh light.

Because America,
I am always firstly the color of my skin,
Secondly my sex,
Thirdly, a conversation had amongst you without me present.

Because America, the gifts of my mind are of less concern to you, than my propensity to
survive all attempts by you to remove me from mattering.

Because America, the promise of beginnings end with insistence.
And of obedience, no idea is worthy of it.

Because at the End, the measure of Life is the accumulation of the distances the mind has
traveled.

Because America's collective mind hasn't traveled that far, I bend
or leap
depending on how high,
or low,
the stick.

Squeezing my multitudes into a passing thinness,
Wallpapered,
Pressed,
Pinned,
My Blackness accenting the unrelenting monotony of white expanses.

Because America,
Body-guarding,
I absorb.
In defiance I stand, knowing I am meant to fall before you.

Because my pain profits you America, you line me up and pick identities for me, and when I die, you
tell my story from the point of the view of you.

Because America proclaims my death to be both Biblically foretold and evidentiary of my predaciousness –

Fertilizer for culture, my value.

My body, your sacrifice.

Because America, fearing
unfettered imagination,
worships protestant elegies to Order.
And you believe your body to be a rental,
And honor the hierarchies of Christendom,
And while collecting revenues from the repeated holy mistakes of history: enslavement and plunder, pillage, and conquer!

Genuflect to Golgotha! And idolize the Palatine.

The un-fucked Holy men dispense merits to those who punish their flesh in the name of Western civilization's obsession with unmaking man's connection to the natural world;

While also believing those without money to be people of the dirt and of the mud,
of reeds and thatch,
of animal skins and insect dyes,
of the forest and farm,
Of chattel and chaff,

the un-moneyed,
closer to nature,
envied for their purity,
pitted for their poverty.

In that story
My blackness is used as an abbreviation for search for life's meaning.

Those Negro streets brimming ripe with Caucasians living the authentic American life of acquisition.

Because America, composted history makes fertile ground for repetitions of all that has been planted before.
Because America, not even the dead are without futures.
Because America, I do not live to die for you

All endings and all beginnings begin and end perceptions and definitions,

Because America, the order of our need circumscribes our life even as they limit our understanding of what is possible:
of what is past,
of what can no longer be,
of what could have been.

Because in this moment America, there is no yesterday more important than the one that just came into existence.

I am, here now, alive.
My sight is clear.
Here and now.
Because America,
What is behind you is evidence.
What is before you is possibility.

Folly believes youth is the same as vitality.

Time instructs that age itself is the master of all things.

And only in time are the knitted strands of identity and purpose, and place and distinction, twisted into a self.

Only then, do we have a face to see.

Here now are my legs and oh, how my arms hang long and low,
Here are my hands, and this is the touch that is kind,
And here now, the touch of desire, of fear, of possession, of deliverance, of surrender, of life –

awake and suffer,
sleep and be unmoved.

Because America, it is the friction that brings presence, and pleasure seems to follow the abrasions.

Because America,
Life is born in friction,
And lived through wars.
And our battles birth our consciousness
Because America,
Life is born in friction,

And lived through wars.

And our battles birth our consciousness.

And of our losses, we sing odes of the heart that hurts,

Of the bodies that are no longer,

And of the eyes that have tired of seeing only that which is outlined by the defeated char-coal,

by the heat of war –

Because America...

Jacksonville, Alabama

Ronnie Festok

This is as far from war
As I'll ever be, among

Gun stores and flea markets,
Hitch-hike and pick-pocket.

The finite is an afternoon
Pastime spent in graveyards

As the air cloys with eulogy
Or simmering heat or church

Bells – I don't recall. I only remember
The taste of honeysuckle fondly,

The spectacle of their unveiling
Desire. Here, everything

Makes a name out of its absence.
Lonicera chrysantha.

Dolly's Craft Store. My mother
And her hijab. What else

Do we keep but our names?
Even this voice will one day wilt –

Forget the dead laughing at us
And our attempts to make a home.

Manhood-Necked Naked Tattered Boy

Asad Ali

I hope my nation is freed someday.
I am very tired and
my neck is manhood.

Let me lay my head back in a garden at midnight.

Right outside of here,
where in desolate apartments, we
realized that there are no mechanics to my voice.

Another strange call:
"There is something you need God to do. Press 1 now, *press 1 now!*"

But even pimps and their whores
understand the physics of paper airplanes.

So do the Jinn, supposedly made of smokeless fire.

The Jinn want to fix the blisters in our feet
from when we wore these dust-colored shoes
like we were *again* or *still* departing from home.

Sometimes I can be farsighted.

I hope your nation *is* someday. To exist is a triumph of our best estimates and
unknowing sighs.

You — human of nation — *are*.
Your rose shine, your verbose apologies to God
your marveling at the Well of Death.
Even your recognition of the scent of my mother's winter embrace.

There are parts for everything these days:
Mowing lawns, kissing foreheads in resignation
Institutes of Design and even paper airplanes.

Paper airplanes, now that tattered and free boys can jump in the sun,
run into small huts, and envy me.

!@$SOLD!@#

Nicholas Luchenbill

Fly

Andres Aguilar

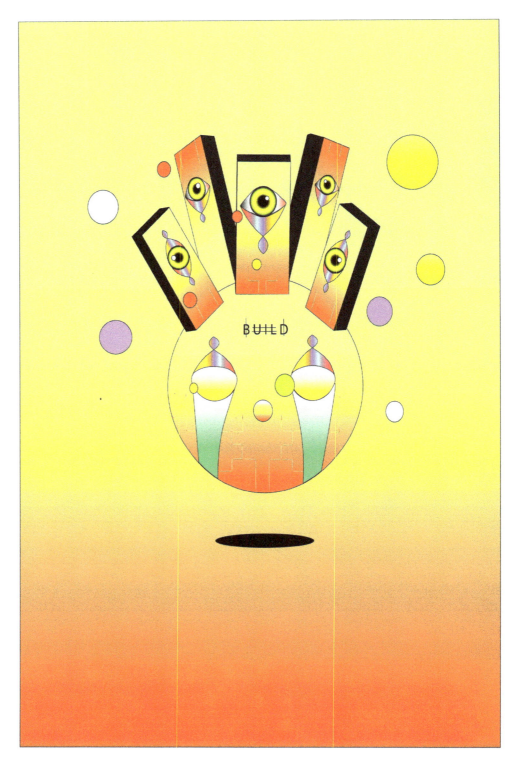

Release Notes for Leonard, 24 Years Old

bp james

Leo v1.2.4 (formerly lil' lick) is now available for deployment in your social environment. This version of Leo (formerly lil' lick) offers a complete rebranding to suit your new and sophisticated young professional lifestyle while continuing to round out your friendship circle as the "self-deprecating goof-ball" companion.

Requirements
Leo v1.2.4 (formerly lil' lick) requires the following to operate in your social environment:

- a cannabis delivery apparatus
- hummus
- hugs

Note: Hugs should be distributed by approved friends. Embraces from strangers and strongly scented elders are not recommended.

New Features
The following features have been added to Leo (formerly lil' lick).

Rebranding:

> Leo, who used to go by "lil' lick", a nick-name coined by the greater online community (and was never approved by marketing) now goes by an abbreviation of his v1.0.0 title, "Leo". You can now introduce Leo to your hip young professional friends under the guise that he, too, is professional.

> Leo now wears tapered chino pants that can be worn in the workplace and hip night-life environments. Black and navy shades are included.

> **Note:** A belt is required. A belt color corresponding to shoe color is preferred.

> Leo also comes with a built-in tattoo on his right forearm, which reads "Good things come to those who wait" in calligraphy. You can ask Leo to talk about the inspiration behind his pop-culture flesh art to fill con—versational gaps in your social environment.

> Leo's "Allison Always" tattoo on his left chest was filled in with a black heart.

Relationships:

> Leo is now single. You can approach him for sage life advice when sober. For jaded "love is folly" monologues in your social environment, add mid-shelf tequila or Jim Beam to your social environment

A future iteration of Leo will support dating, mingling, and charm.

Note: Attempting to change Leo's relationship state (also known as "set—ting up" or "wing-manning") is not recommended and may cause Leo's confidence configuration to return error.

Faith:

Leo is now vocal about his identity as spiritual but not Christian. You can prompt Leo to expand on this feature with biblical text, ghost stories, and hot takes about the origin of the cosmos.

Employment:

Leo v.1.2.4 now maintains a full-time job in waste management, a feature previously deprecated in v1.2.2. With the return of a steady income, you can now invite Leo to fast casual restaurants, budget films, and mini golf.

Leo also has health insurance, 10 days of paid time-off per year, and a parking pass for the parking ramp at the corner of 3rd and Washington.

Hobbies:

As a result of the existential crisis triggered by his break-up, Leo has latched on to the following hobbies to feel whole:

- Photography
- Drink coaster collecting
- Cooking documentaries

These hobbies are merely a phase of coping and should not be considered a permanent addition to your social environment. A future iteration of Leo will include interests more synonymous with Leo's identity. You can follow Leo's Instagram account, which includes photos from his hikes and the occasional insta-poem caption, by searching his handle *@lillick*.

Note: A future iteration of Leo will include a rebranded Instagram handle.

Bug Fixes
Leo v1.2.4 includes the following bug fixes:

- Leo no longer flosses in public.
- Leo no longer leaves peanut butter caked knives at the bottom of sinks.
- Leo's ring worm on his upper-back has been deprecated.

- Leo consistently remembers to bring his ID to bars and R-rated films.
- Leo now consults nearby adults before clicking on phishing emails.

Known Issues

The following issues are known with Leo:

Note: Due to the extensive list of issues, only the most common and crippling issues are listed.

- Leo may forget to buy his mother a birthday present.
- Sometimes, Leo initiates handshakes with his left hand.
- Leo does not utilize overdraft protection on his checking account.
- Leo may not receive emojis on his iPhone 4 due to iOS compatibility issues.
- Leo does not recycle.
- When pouring a beer, Leo may forget to tilt the glass and allow foam to overflow.
- If given DJ privileges in a vehicle or home stereo environment, Leo may play dastardly artists such as Yelawolf, Carly Rae Jepson deep tracks, and Art Garfunkel.
- Leo cannot operate self-checkout aisles at grocery stores.
- When talking to women, Leo may lie about his education and shoe size.
- Sometimes, Leo may produce and present unwanted and generally unimpressive poetry to his social environment when using cannabis.
- To access his email, Leo must reset his password each time since he cannot remember.
- Leo fails to support house plants.

For more information on deploying Leo in your social environment, contact Leo Support.

implications of a midmorning sunset

Riley Lopez

violets are alone,
though they grow in clusters,
unbidden in meadows,
unmatched in their loveliness.
loosely, but surely, the breeze
tugs them westward.

the morning warmth recedes,
calling on the evening much too soon,
leaving dew,
draining color,
stitching mournful quilts of shade.

this premature and tender darkness is a prayer
spoken by someone who's had you on his mind.

The Peony and the Ant

Josephine Pino

Globe swollen
petal laden, I welcome
your symbiotic
caress

Your sly explorations
conjure emerging
dew, a
nectar gleam

inducing your eager
lapping, your
body a curl to
match my curve.

My need to give
feeds your need to
shield against
armoured buzz.

Blushing beneath
staccato shadow and
quilted skies, I burst forth
in glorious bloom.

My bud opens
splashing red
and you depart,
stinger sheathed

The Intuitive Collection

Jenn Conley

Predatory Arthropod

Tamara MC

I.

I am opportunistic. I have eight legs, a grasping claw, and a segmented tail. My back curves. I come out at night to hunt. I bury in the undersides of rocks and in sand. I don't peek my head forth until I see an enemy approaching. I hide in corners on bare Saltillo tile floors. Kids find me with their hands, but it is too late. I have already stung them. I am Scorpion. I sting. Venom comes from my claws, my mouth, and a stinger on my ass, like the bumblebee you met when you were twelve. But don't mistake me. I don't bumble. I kill and paralyze my prey. My mixture of neurotoxins and enzyme inhibitors is fast acting. I turn my victims to liquid.

I suck them dry.

I crush.

I hiss.

II.
You were kindness. You were stable. You were balanced. Your hard shell kept me unwavering. Your strength, elevating me.

You courted me in a *promenade à deux*. You led me with a juddering kiss—your clawlike mouth grasping my pincers and injecting me with a pacifying venom. You searched for a suitable place to deposit yourself. You, in a hurry. You didn't want me to lose interest for fear I may cannibalize you.
my hat on through Communion and Blessings.

III.

Your mother carried you on her back. You depended on her moisture.
You resemble her—
You had a choice to protect from evil or be an embodiment of evil. You chose the latter.

You used your slitted, circular, elliptical and oval eyes—the two on the top of your skull,
and the five pairs along the front corners of your head to stalk me.

Your two tails, a genetic abnormality were needed to sufficiently paralyze me.

I needed the sting. I needed it hard and long. I needed to learn not to trust.
I took the sting not once but for many for many, many years.
You saw innocence. You saw hidden frailty. You saw Nazi's behind my blind eyes.

You knew you could be the Hitler in my life.

IV.

Mate to Scorpion:
A scorpion will always be a scorpion. Your outer shell will never reveal the softness I thought I found. It is lost. You are lost. You cannot be the moulted scorpion I need. You still have to work on the Amma and Abba in your life. You still need to work on Oni. When her high heels jabbed you in your tender child ribs, you got lost in that closet. You will never recover from, "I hate you. I wish I never had a Scorpion son like you." Not in this life, Tan. Not now. You must be reincarnated to find your way. You may think you have found it in this lifetime, but don't be fooled.

Scorpion to Mate:
You are wise. Use your analytical mind. Not your heart. It will not lead you wrong. I leave you with such sadness. I have known nothing other than your breath. You were my first love. And you will always be my only real love. Our love is evidenced in our boys. They came from you and learned the lessons I wasn't taught. Their shell is much softer than mine. Follow your boys. Let them listen to you cry. Let them be men. Let them do their own laundry. I'll always need your voice to put me to sleep. I will always prefer your chicken curry to my mom's. Never think this is about you. It is all about me. It always was. You will learn to trust again.

You may die early but you will have lived your life like Hitler asked you to do.

God bless you Tamara and may you rest in peace.

V.

Mate to Scorpion:
You haven't yet shedded your exoskeleton. Your instars haven't molted into maturity yet. You will emerge when this split takes place. You will become soft and stretch into your new body.

Scorpion to Mate:
In your next life, look for two black rocks surrounded by white sand and you will find me.

Sky/Sounds

Lynn Hanley

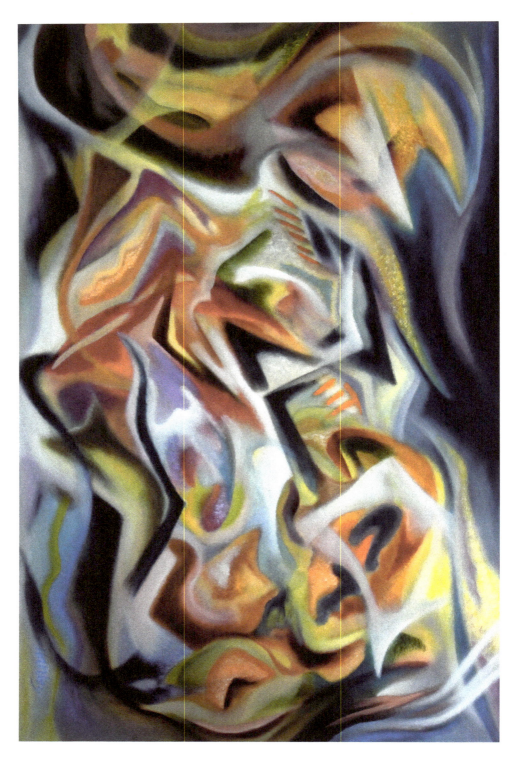

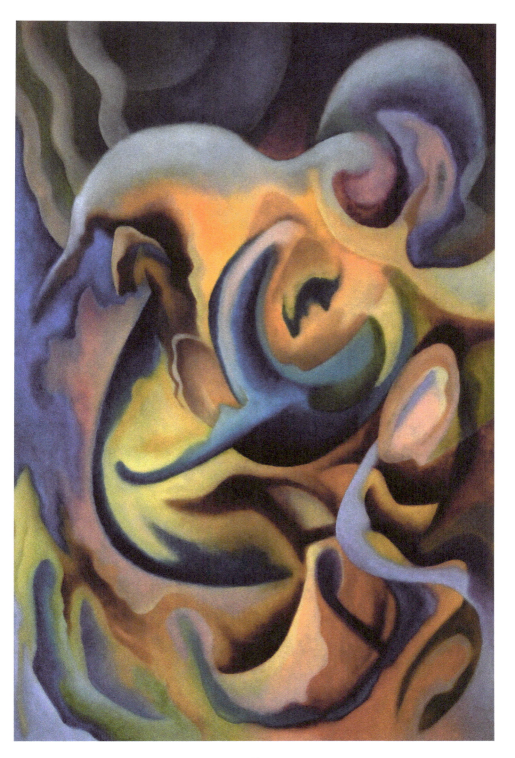

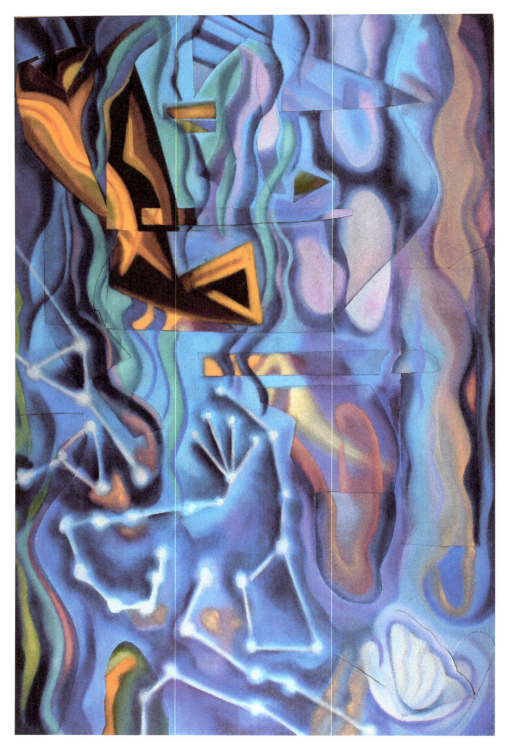

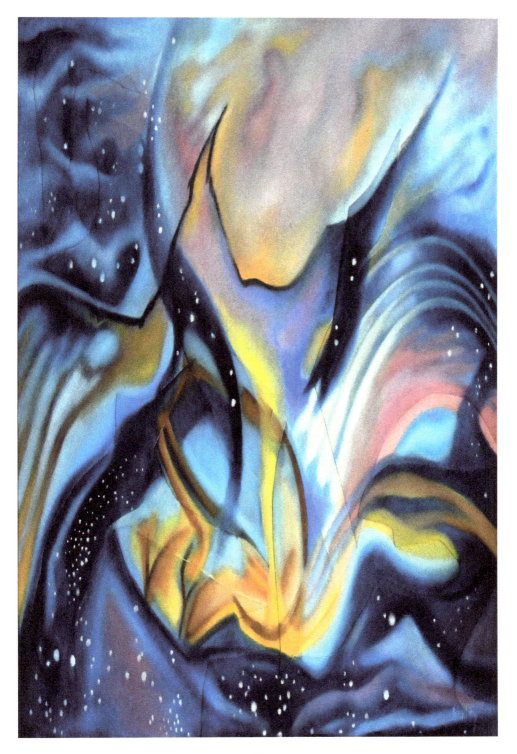

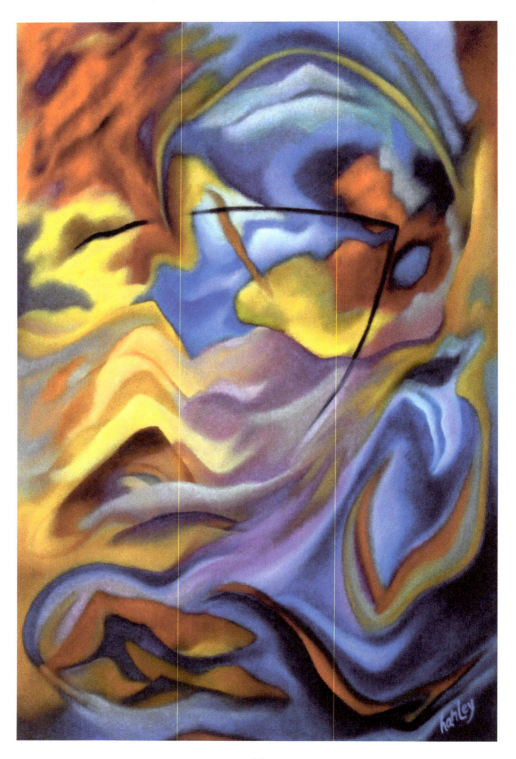

46

POSTMORTEM

Meghan Tanaka

There she is, in the waking.
Quiet sputter. Quiet heart.
Miles of memory hang
like tinsel on a dozen ribs.
Beneath the stillness
blows a pink wind.
The crying born in summer,
in a dirty street, bug-lit
on a small skinned knee.
Baby fat & red, runny nose.
The crying stopped in a bedroom,
in a limp blue blanket. One hand
on a husband, one on the heart.
At least the husband was there.
At least there was love
like a mug in December.
Warm waiting. Quick snow.

The House Fell

Josie Turner

It was like an earthquake. That shaking begins, crashing noise you don't hear
coming from anywhere, shaking rattles, continues,
        until you cannot think anymore. It is that kind of shaking
I hear and feel when I see a motorcyclist on a rainy day.
I remember the artist, Michael Fajans, and it is that kind of shaking
I think about when you leave in the morning, and I know
I have not a rational reason to worry but I do worry, will you come home?
It does not make sense, but it is what I think about.
I think about the person who at Michael's funeral described
        how there was blood coming out of his mouth,
I wondered if the red was a red he would have liked, like the red on his paintings
        the painting at the airport,
I wish I could be his magician and pull him out of a hat, make him whole again
        like Michael painted the magician and his rabbit.
I did not even know Michael. But Bill, you and your paint,
        he was a painter and your friend.
I put tomatoes into the fish stew pot, they gurgle, bubble and mix around
        cilantro, olive oil, wine. They are my creation, my work of art
           my wanting to feed you, my wanting to feed myself, mother myself.

****

My mother did not allow me to suckle -
mothers in the 1950's found suckling old fashioned
like making cake from scratch. Cake came
from a Betty Crocker box, the kind one egg
was added, and then it became scratch. She
scratched my scratched hand, and the scab
came off but it was not a scab on my hand as much
as in my ears. Ringing, ringing, my Mother's screaming.
I dive into, under, the water hold my breath until
I am forced to re-enter and hear hysteria.
I dive below again hoping it stops, and it never does.
She puts black patent leather shoes on my feet,
white socks with lace and ruffles, turns me around.

I am stiff, like a corpse, quaking.
I do not move until the clash, bang, the symbol
that it is OK to move, before I curtsey.
My cheeks, red from cortisone, steroid puffy,
stiff, and stumbling, petticoats rustling, layers of tulle lined
satin lined, elastic lined under my chin, holding
my hat on through Communion and Blessings.

****

I am holding on.
There is no other sibling. The doctors look at me
  as if that is my fault, it might as well be.
No other to look after her, whose dreams
  changed and faded a red sky morning
  only to look and tell what the night before might have held.
Maybe it is I who needs the happy pills, the elixirs
  to cure the quaking inside my stomach each time
I get the phone call to stop, remain. Still I come running
  give her oxygen, count blessings that it is not you,
  dreading the time when it may be you.
I look away every time that needle is inserted into delicate
  freckled, thin skin, watching the blood spurt out,
  up and hating every time someone says
  your mother, she's so nice, she's so loving.
  If they only knew that loving was controlling.
I wait, remain controlled, hearing the latest diagnosis.

I stand waiting for the dancing to stop.
The great aunts are lined against a wall, linear.
Their hair all the same height, their hands folded
  across their laps, their laps lined flatly,
  tucked in firmly by girdles and corsets.
My mother takes my hand, hurries, jerking, twirling
me around, and I land on a great aunt's
  black laced shoe. Petticoats exposed, panties exposed
  showing quality of make, brand.

I have been exposed, branded perfect, each hair in place,
        loving put in place, better than the cousins' hair in place.
My mother put my hair in place. It is that picture,
        the one you cannot stand, the one in which we all stand.
My mother and her sisters, my father, my uncles,
        my grandmother, my grandfather, my cousins
        all six of them, and me, and you say you
        have never seen a group of less happy people,
        and the youngest cousin, he's squirming.
I can tell even now though it was over 45 years ago,
        squirming afraid of a belted earthquake crack.
I am looking through the crack, the one not in the picture,
        the one between the closed blinds, looking out to white sand,
        ocean, feeling the coming tidal wave crashing.

****

The latest gift of love crashed onto the floor
shattered into thousands of pieces, shattered not
to be glued back. I have no children to shatter, glue,
only you, Mom, keeping you pieced together, piece by piece
while in my mind I hear silent white space, the notes,
whole notes, resting, at peace. The fault widens,
closes, changes by the day, was it mine, yours?
Fish stew bubbles boils on the stove, blood like red
stew. I stir it. The clock ticks, its hands against
a smiling elephant, silent, hanging on the plastered wall.

Mom looks at me. *I don't know, just don't,*
just can never understand how you learned to cook.
Your grandmother did not cook,
your great-grandmother did not cook,
there were cooks.
    Dad cooked, I say. *Not well,*
        she says. *He only thought he could cook.*
Oh, I say. *Maybe then it was out of survival.*
What I don't say is how my friend who was gay
taught me to cook, cook when we were early in college,

52

stirring sauces, glazes, glacé fruit, chocolate mousse.
It was a must, my only way, way to make any sense of anything,
a place to hide, be an artist. Yes, the dirty word artist,
we do survive Mom, we do survive, not holding still.
It was the earthquake that blew my husband
out of his fortress, his studio. I watched him as he flew,
not like Chagall's angels, violins over villages, but flying into paint,
plump picture-perfect paint, painting me, painting blue.
I don't think he will ever paint you.

Network your Way to Writerly Success!!

Julie Benesh

Like with everything else, writing is far less about what you know than WHO you manage to startle into submission. So sharpen those writing implements and let's go!

1. Prioritize. You are likely spending way too much time writing. Use the "80-20 rule," For every 20 words, you write, send out 80 "aspirational" query letters. That will keep you motivated and on track. And don't waste energy *writing* the letters--templates are available (for a nominal fee--see my **website**), and it's safest to keep it generic at this point, anyway, at least until you have a "piece" of "writing" to, you know, write about.

2. Get out there! No writer ever became successful by sitting at home... writing. There are so many literary events just waiting for you to showcase your potential authordom. The problem is, until you are "established," they won't be asking you to keynote. It's one of those frustrating "chicken-egg" situations, (to coin a writerly phrase). That means you must learn to a) hijack readings (e.g., simply muscle your way to the stage just before the applause dies out) and b) stowaway at those pricey conferences (remember, cater-waiter jobs have high turnover and literary gatekeepers love to eat and drink).

3. Once you are in the door, you need to stand out in the crowd (to coin some more writerly phrases). You may never be as powerfully athletic as Joyce Carol Oates, or even as smooth and hairless as Stephen King. But you must have some kind of eccentric charm you can exploit for the cause. Think back to your grade school talent show or your most uncomfortable medical exam. Dig deep! Or, if you must, take some of that wasted "writing" time and teach yourself to hacky-sack with bookends or something equally literary.

4. Once you get hacking, what's a writer without a line—get it? Master the art of "negging." When you do meet an eligible editor or agent, make a witty comment deprecating a recent publication, one of their so-called authors, or their hairstyle or lack thereof. It works great for picking up chicks and it'll also get you published! (Join my exclusive Neg-a-Day **mailing list** –see my **website** for information.)

5. Speaking of meat markets, a picture is worth a thousand words, so invest in a professional headshot. Of your good-looking cousin, I mean. If your cousin is not quite camera-ready, you may think you can just snag something off the web, but most headshots lack the necessary cupped hands and soulful, faraway expression in the eyes. (See my exclusive **website** offer for a helpfully curated collection of a full range of genres-- feel free to just photoshop your

own best feature onto any one of them like a B+-list parent cheating a sub-Ivy Admissions counselor.)

6. Also, spend the money, and further prove your dedication by risking physical harm, to 3-D print yourself (or your cousin) for those busy days, nights and weeks when Literary Events are occurring and you can't be everywhere in person at once. If your insurance won't cover this procedure, a limited edition of Literary Mannequins is also available on my **website**.

7. Consider Artificial Intelligence to take your 3D game to the Next Level. Program in your fav negs, or the whole 365! (You know where to find those! On my **website**, I mean.)

8. Follow up! Now that you (or your 3D image, mannequin, or robot) are everywhere you need to be looking good and talking down, you need to follow up to make that dazzling first impression last! Create a set of email responses and robo-calls designed to never, ever let them forget about you. Consider a clever "Don't You forget About Me" GIF! (Other equally sophisticated and nuanced ideas on my **website**, or for a nominal fee we can customize something just for you!)

9. Whatever you or your …er, team…do, always remember, it's not about you and what you want and those editors an agents doing a favor for you. It's all about what you can do for them-- so you better let them know who's boss!

10. Did I mention I have a **website**? You should maybe get a **website**. See my **website** and join my mailing list!

To summarize: It's never about the writing, so knock it off. Spam is delicious. Hijack the competition. Cultivate ubiquity and eccentricity. Exploit cousins and robots. Remember, it's about covering up our bland social awkwardness with a dash of obnoxiousness, so we got this! Always judge an author by their **website**. Visit my **website**.

However, and with Great Sincerity...

Ivan Marquez

E-mail received by CICC Office Dated
10/18/2001–FWD: FWD: FWD: URGENT!!!!!!

To Whom It May Concern:

This is Dick Ellerbe writing on behalf of Colesqua High School with regard to the proctor booklets that were distributed to our district office this past week. The content of the booklets does not seem aligned to the State Standardized Test and deviates wildly in terms of content and decency. There must have been a massive oversight on your end and–believe you me–I will walk through hell's boiler room to ensure that the heads of high-ranking officers in your department are rolling down central office halls or placed atop pikes along I-57 for this unnecessary emergency.

Since no one in your office can be bothered to proofread what you send out, attached are some of the excerpts (the ones that made some semblance of coherent thought).

Also, my suggestion to amend the situation would be a new set of appropriate booklets sent first class to our district office before test day and for you all to kiss my ass. A picture of which has been faxed to your office.

I am awaiting the booklets.

Dr. Dick Ellerbe Ph.Ed
Assistant Principal
Colesqua High-School

— .— —.— . / —— —.—— / .... .— —. —.. .—.—.— / — .... / .. ... / —— ..— .—. / —... . ——. .. —. —. .. —. ——.

Ahead of Testing Day or Hwaet! We Gardena   in geardagum.... (Virgil)

You will be proctoring the Practice Standard Aptitude Exam. This test book-let was provided to you by the state of Illinois in accordance with the standards and practices set forth by the Committee of Central Illinois Colleges (a regional branch of the College Board). All directions have been approved by a Board-Certified Member[1] in accordance with Illinois State and Federal law.

Please take a moment to familiarize yourself with the glossary located on page 64 of your Proctor Booklet. It is important that you understand the terms used throughout the testing booklet before testing day.

This is your assigned guide for administering the PSAE. Take a moment to read and remember your guide's name, as it will be imperative on test day. The Guide's name is located in the parentheses of this section's title.

Although you have already spent the two weeks preparing for the test, which included countless formal and informal conversations as well as two PLP's that could have been condensed to an e-mail, please take a moment to forget them, as all that you will need is between these covers. Please go over your test day scripts so that you may clarify any questions you may have with your test day administrative team.

On Test Day, Proctors will need to be:

- Well versed in the exam and all aspects of its administration. It is vital that all proctors know what to expect on test day.
- Assigned a classroom to proctor as well as a sheet of student names listed in alphabetical order. Note: though your roster is in alphabetical order, students should be seated randomly throughout the room. A seating chart has been provided to you by the CIC.
- Gallant (Please take a moment to familiarize yourself with the C.I.C definition located on page 64 of your proctor booklet).
- Well stocked with #2 pencils.

[1] It should be stated that the SAE technical writer's manual forbids writers from using footnotes to distrib-ute any information as it may be confusing for proctors during testing day. This quote can be found in the lone footnote of the manual in section SS. 342.64*. Technical writers are the freaks of the writing world as we are the few whose job entails removing all voice from our writing; we need only disseminate information as simply and clearly as possible. This brought both awe and suspicion to technical writers as we could not discern whether the footnote was meant to create confusion-- thus providing a valuable lesson through example-- or was an act of defiance. The debate still continues in Tech Writing circles, with practitioners falling into the two previously mentioned camps. I am of the latter, choosing to paint and inscribe my name on the bars that block my view.

Take a moment to familiarize yourself with your class roster. Make sure that you are proctoring a class that you do not teach. For example, a Junior level teacher should not proctor a Junior level test as there may be a conflict of interest. Since tests scores weigh heavily on the employment decisions made for the following school year, it is important that students know and understand the importance of the exam and that the importance of this exam has been communicated to them by others prior to test day.

Any irregularities should be recorded in the irregularity report found in the back of the proctor booklet.

Boredom is to be expected and should be recorded in your irregularity report. Students may look around and out of windows, wishing to be anywhere else except within that room. Wishing to be anywhere else. Wishing to be anyone else. Remind students to face forward as the PSAE testing room is no place for existential ennui[2].

Ensure that twins are actually twins and not doppelgängers[3]. If you are not sure, and there is no way to tell, seat them far apart from one another and away from the other's sight, as one will assume the identity of the other.

Students should be well aware that the results of this test will haunt them as the specter of Marx haunts Europe—a decision made in their past will inform their every decision moving forward. Some may feel that upon graduation they have moved on from the test and that the results no longer reflect their value or spotty character.

They are sorely mistaken.

Students may ask to use the restroom. Do not let them go unless it is an emergency. If the student leaves, make sure that you remove the test from their desk and keep it near you and away from the prying, weasely eyes of test takers. Students become more daring when their backs are against the wall and even the most mild-mannered student will bend or break regulation to keep the specter of failure at bay—or at arm's length. Though students are allowed to use the restroom, they are not allowed to do so to vomit. Vomiting is a natural occurrence to a body under extreme amounts of stress and does not constitute any emergency, medical or otherwise. Please place a small paper bag at the foot of each students' desk.

[2]Apathy and irony are the parents of adolescent melancholy and they will take students by each hand and walk them through life. Life no longer becomes something that happens to you, but around you; An audience to the world's stage, being shut out of all that light.

[3]One may recall "the doubles" incident that took place in Madison, Wisconsin during the 1981 testing season where, after hours of rigorous testing that led to multiple pencils broken or worked to the eraser's nub, saw the district receive multiple phone calls of parents claiming that their children didn't "appear the same". Not that they looked different, but that there was a certain hollowness to them, a slight difference that could be felt but not seen, heard within the inflection of their voices, but difficult to describe. The Madison district of course promised that the people occupying their homes were, in fact, their students and that they had just undergone extreme stress from testing, reassuring them not to worry and that their child would return to normal in "no time at all" (though one administrator used the term "jiffy", which he felt was inappropriate).The origin of these doubles is split between two camps. The first being the high population of Germans within your region. It is a well recorded fact that a population can bring their specters with them—carried within the collective their subconscious and sprung forth in times of great distress. The second is that the stress of the SAE causes a split within the student, IE the energy from within the student manifests itself outside the student, thus forcing the student to literally confront themselves. It is a battle seldom won, for who can honestly face themselves?

Daydreaming should be documented in your irregularity report. There are no dreams within the testing rooms as dreams connote *Hope* (Please refer to the C.I.C definition located on page 64 of your proctor booklet). The test is meant for students to confront their limitations, to push them to the metaphorical edge by the nape of the neck, forcing them to look at what lies beneath them should they fail: a great falling with no safety net or communal hand to save them. It is not uncommon for students to hallucinate that the entire class has vanished and that they are the only ones left in the room or for the room to change dimensions anytime they look up to check their time. Though the test is taken with others, it is a confirmation of the solipsist's delusion.

Remind students that they are alone[4].

Also, remind students calmly, however with great sincerity, that they will require a #2 pencil.

. . -.. .. / . . -.. .. / . -.. . - -- . - / .... . - -... . - -. -. .... - .... . - -. .. .. --..

On Test Day

Students should know the importance of this exam. The importance should have been stressed in the weeks leading up to test day. If the student does not take the test seriously, there is something wrong with that student's *Moral Compass* (Please take a moment to familiarize yourself with the C.I.C definition located on page 64 of your proctor booklet). Students who choose not to take the test seriously should have their name and ID numbers recorded on the irregularity report and should be escorted from the testing room in hand-cuffs.

Take a moment to look into the figurative and metaphoric *Heart (The definition of which is inscribed on the walls of your own)* of each Student. Ensure that they are (1) *True* (Please take a moment to familiarize yourself with the C.I.C definition located on page 64 of your proctor booklet) and (2) *Pure* (Please take a moment to familiarize yourself with the C.I.C definition located on page 64 of your proctor booklet). Continue if, and only if, all students fit this description. If student(s) does not fit the description, please have your administrative team contact the College Board.

-- . -- --- . -. -. -- / .. ... / . - / ... -. --- . -- / -. -. . -. . - ... - . . -.. / .. - . .. . . -. - -..

---

[4]The SAE—the standardized test your students are preparing for—is the last great communal challenge these students will experience together: rows of heads slouched and slumped over bubble sheets, the unbearable stench of stress sweat exasperated by the broken public school A/C or the administrative decision to keep the system off until weather stabilizes, the cut of phlegm cleared and collected in the jowls followed by a soft swallow as students try to concentrate, all while a silent fart prowls the aisles like the 10th plague. Students will wish to escape this not knowing what awaits them. What awaits them after the graduation caps have been removed and flung skyward, after hugs and promises to keep in touch have been exchanged, and bags either packed for college (which only prolongs adolescence) is the world. A world unfair in its ability to tear one down after allowing for great heights. A world of impossible expectations, demanding more than one can give, providing only what one deserves. These post-secondary trials and tribulations are private hells. Look around. Some of your students will not make it to thirty. Some will be confined within cubicles and quietly wish they hadn't. Proctor, take stock in this: though it pains us to be together, we cannot be alone.

Students should be seated in their assigned seats. Tell students that they will be tested on the mastery of the State Standards in compliance with the state of Illinois; the Central Illinois College Board; and the National and Federal Board of Education.

The test will be broken into four sections and timed accordingly.

Writing (55 minutes)

Mathematics (40 minutes)

Science (45 minutes)

Reading (55 minutes)

Writing

Students will be asked to write a personal anecdote about the worst day of their life. Student responses will be read and pondered by the college board and will be graded on whether the student's life is worth living.

Mathematics

Students will be asked to answer questions based on the trajectory of paper airplanes and rocks thrown from the top of the Sears tower. Students will be asked to identify the fall rate as well as the distance traveled given certain wind and air resistance.

Science

Students will be asked a Y/N question on their belief of climate change. Their responses will be measured against their written responses to the reading portion of the test and the college board will make a decision on whether or not students are true reflections of the state.

Reading

For the reading portion of the exam, students will answer questions on the forced migration of Illinois Native-Americans to the western border of Kansas at the hands of the federal government led by General Steve Miller[5]. The reading will have students identify dependent and independent clauses and how the deployment of semi-

---

[5]Produced by the state and completely centered around the Gen. Miller, the story does not cover the much more harrowing journey of a family of three who saw the father executed just outside of the town center by Gen. Miller himself prior to the march. The mother, who had left much of the decision making up to the family patriarch, now needed to defend the life of herself and her very young daughter. Who marched through the central Illinois cold, their only wish to stop walking while whispering stories that are now long forgotten through chattering teeth, her words carried by chilled December breath beneath a gray sky that allowed no sun. Who would have their wish granted on December 27th as the two lay clasped and covered by snow, left behind by Gen. Miller, never to have a blot of ink spilled in their name.

colons, colons, and commas further strengthens the relationship between clauses and justifies the forced migration of a people across a country in the dead of winter. Students will be asked to reflect on the *Gallantry* of Gen. Miller and how his stoic *courage* helped clear the land for American settlers moving west in fulfillment of their god given right to the prairie lands. Students will also be asked of how Gen. Miller is the embodiment of Illinois and Mid-Western Values[6].

****

Now say calmly, however with great sincerity...

"Open your testing booklet to page six. Do not move ahead of this section or your test will be void. You will have 55 minutes to complete the Reading portion of the exam. Your time starts now. Good luck."

---

[6]The extent of the violence sanctioned by the state is veiled by language and framed within the margin of the page. It's the state's confession laid bare before apathetic eyes that hallucinate and dart between page and clock. A confession of violence in the name of manifest destiny is still a confession of violence and the state litters the test with these pedantic whispers. The key is awareness, proctor. What is needed is not ironic detachment, but true unspoken courage. The courage to rise in the face of impossible expectations and be cut down, day in and day out, only to rise and return again, like living revenants, not because life is meaningless, but in spite of it.

Heart-to-Heart

Photography by Kevin Morris
Poetry by Devon Balwit

She won't have children, she says, as we watch
another's child taunt the surf, all bright
shrieks at the waves' skirmishes. What
of the plastic vortex, she asks, or the smudge

of stars gone from the night? And the water table
retreating along with the glaciers, whole cities
left bone dry? I get her acerbity.
My generation messed up, unable

to look beyond its mown lawns, its love
of more. I watch the boy, light-haloed,
conch in hand a trumpet. He is loud,
oblivious to being among the last to move

on two feet. I hope she'll change her mind,
but what convincing argument can I find?

In Order Of Appearance:

Beth SK Morris is the author of two poetry books: "Nowhere to be Found" (2014) and "In Florida (2010). Her poems have appeared in Artemis, Avocet, Broadkill Review, Crosswinds, Pank, and Poetica, online in Screw Iowa! and Bridle Path Press among others. Beth is a member of the Hudson Valley Writers Center and Poets House in New York.

Jeremiah Gilbert is an award-winning photographer and avid traveler. He likes to travel light and shoot handheld. His travels have taken him to over eighty countries and territories spread across five continents. His photography has been published internationally, in both digital and print publications, and has been exhibited worldwide. His travel tales and portfolio can be found at www.jeremiahgilbert.com.

Richard Stuart Perkins (b. Oklahoma, USA) is a writer, photographer and painter living in New York, whose works examine the importance of remembering and forgetting, of memory, of the social, sexual, political conflicts and contradictions that animate his life. He seeks through poetry to speak of the collective struggles we face forging individual identities in the midst of socially dictated concepts of race, gender, and sexuality. The poems in Everyone Is There When We Look, the manuscript submitted here concern Race, Gender, Sexuality, and Age. The poems also address the roles history, tradition, religion and government play in the creation of both individual and collective mythologies regarding a person, a culture, a place and a time.

Ronnie Festok is a Syrian-American who grew up in Birmingham, Alabama. He is currently a junior at Emory University and has work published in Vinyl.

Asad Ali is a Pakistani-American writer and current undergraduate at the University of Virginia. His style of writing revolves around the deconstruction and abstraction of the ghazal, a sonnet-like form of poetry originating in 7th century Arabia, as it has been used in the South Asian context (e.g., Urdu poetry). Ali's work has previously been published in Flux Magazine at the University of Virginia and the A3 Review.

Nicholas Luchenbill (born 1983, Michigan) is a Texas-based photographer and visual artist. After high school, Nicholas joined the United States Army where he served 10 years active duty, and three combat tours in the middle east. Nicholas uses his photographic practice in understanding his own wounds from war trauma, and also to speak to other Veterans that are suffering from PTSD, with a primary focus on the mental health issues surrounding the Veteran community.

Andres was born in Canada, spending most of his time writing in any type of genre and drawing in any type of form. Andres also has a poetry book published on Kobo.

bp james is a writer and observationist from Northwestern Wisconsin.

Riley Lopez was born in Maryland to a Cuban-Irish household, but now lives, writes, and learns in New York City. His work has previously appeared in Yes Poetry and Impossible Archetype: A Journal of LGBTQ+ Poetry. He was also a finalist in the Brooklyn Poets Whitman Bicentennial Poetry Contest.

Josephine is an educator who continues to explore the ways that poetry, teaching and Biology not only play well together, they help each other thrive. She has published in El Portal, Cathexis NW, Curating Alexandria, and Raw Art Review, and featured in High Shelf and Tiny Seed Literary Journal.

Jenn Conley is an acrylic artist from South Jersey. You can find more of her art on Facebook and Instagram.
www.instagram.com/jenncbinspired/
www.facebook.com/JennConleyBInspired/

Dr. Tamara MC is an Applied Linguist and focuses on issues related to language, culture, and identity in the Middle East and beyond, specifically her hybrid and juxtaposed identity of growing up simultaneously Jewish and Muslim in a Sufi commune in Texas. She has various publications in journals such as, the Berkeley Poetry Review, OVS Magazine, Fiction International, Sand Script, Poetica Magazine, Driftwood Press, Sling Magazine, and Blue Guitar. She attended residencies at such places as, The Iowa Writers' Workshop Summer Program, BreadLoaf, Sewanee, Summer Literary Seminars in Lithuania, and Naropa. She has also been awarded fellowships at Ragdale, Los Angeles Review of Books/University of Southern California Publishing Workshop, Virginia Center for the Creative Arts, Vermont Studio Center, Community of Writers at Squaw Valley, and others. She has taught as full-time faculty at the the University of Arizona, both ESL and teacher training classes. She most recently was an English Language Fellow for the U.S. Department of State and Georgetown University in Tbilisi, Georgia with the Shota Rustaveli Theatre and Film Georgia State University. When she isn't teaching or writing, she is creating three-dimensional art with found materials or running marathons. She is a mama to two amazing sons and an adorable Boston Terrier named Blazer.

As a working artist Lynn has had many opportunities to share her creativity. She had the pleasure of creating several exterior murals, one funded by the National Endowment for the Arts. At a liberal arts college Lynn taught fine art and film for twelve years. Her skills were honed by working as an automotive draftsman for several years. She also taught children in art intensive programs over the summer months. Lynn's passion is to bring beauty into the world. Our universe is filled with grace and she would want very much for her art to be part of that expression.

Meghan Tanaka is from Jackson, MS. She is a recent graduate of the University of Mississippi, where she studied English and philosophy. She enjoys walking her dog and eating cake.

Josie Emmons Turner lives in Tacoma, Washington and is Tacoma's former Poet Laureate. She is the editor of the chapbook "Sarasvati Takes Pegasus as Her Mount" and her work has appeared in California Quarterly, Floating Bridge Review, Creative Colloquy, in Tahoma's Shadow and other journals. She teaches poetry and literature to seniors at Clover Park High School and earned her MFA from the Rainier Writing Workshop at Pacific Lutheran University. *This poem first appeared in an incomplete form in Issue IX

Julie Benesh has been published in Tin House Magazine, Bestial Noise: A Tin House Fiction Reader, Crab Orchard Review, Florida Review, Gulf Stream, Berkeley Fiction Review, Journal of Compressed Creative Arts, Bridge, Green Briar Review, and other places. Julie earned an MFA in fiction from Warren Wilson College, lives in Chicago, and has a day job as a professor and administrator at a school of psychology.

Ivan Marquez is an emerging writer from Illinois. He has been published by Rumble Fish Quarterly.

Kevin Morris blends together wonder and joy; nature and humanity to produce photographs which will ignite your wanderlust for Southern California beaches and nostalgic childhood memories. When he is not capturing moments on his camera, he is typically found hiking, or near the ocean with his wife and son.

Devon Balwit's most recent collection is titled A Brief Way to Identify a Body (Ursus Americanus Press). Her individual poems can be found in Relief: A Journal of Art and Faith, The Cincinnati Review, Tampa Review, Apt (long-form issue), Free State Review, Timberline Review, Rattle, and more. Her books, book reviews, and online work can be found at:
https://pelapdx.wixsite.com/devonbalwitpoet

Highshelfpress.com

CPSIA information can be obtained
at www.ICGtesting.com
Printed in the USA
BVHW020106100919
557955BV00021BA/404/P